Perritos/Dogs

Pugs/Pugs

por/by Jody Sullivan Rake

Traducción/Translation: Dr. Martín Luis Guzmán Ferrer
Editor Consultor/Consulting Editor: Dra. Gail Saunders-Smith

Consultor/Consultant: Jennifer Zablotny, DVM
Member, American Veterinary Medical Association

Mankato, Minnesota

Pebble is published by Capstone Press,
151 Good Counsel Drive, P.O. Box 669, Mankato, Minnesota 56002.
www.capstonepress.com

1 2 3 4 5 6 13 12 11 10 09 08

Library of Congress Cataloging-in-Publication Data
Rake, Jody Sullivan.
    Pugs / por Jody Sullivan Rake = Pugs / by Jody Sullivan Rake.
    p. cm. — (Pebble. Perritos = Pebble. Dogs)
    ISBN-13: 978-1-4296-2386-5 (hardcover)
    ISBN-10: 1-4296-2386-1 (hardcover)
    1. Pug — Juvenile literature. I. Title. II. Series.
SF429.P9R3518 2009
636.76 — dc22   2008001262

Summary: Simple text and photographs present an introduction to the pug breed,
    its growth from puppy to adult, and pet care information — in both English
    and Spanish.

Note to Parents and Teachers

The Perritos/Dogs set supports national science standards related
to life science. This book describes and illustrates pugs in both
English and Spanish. The images support early readers in
understanding the text. The repetition of words and phrases helps
early readers learn new words. This book also introduces early
readers to subject-specific vocabulary words, which are defined
in the Glossary section. Early readers may need assistance to read
some words and to use the Table of Contents, Glossary, Internet
Sites, and Index sections of the book.

Table of Contents

Tabla de contenidos

Brave Dogs

Pugs are brave dogs.

They are not afraid of much,

even though they are small.

Perros valientes

Los pugs son perros valientes.

A pesar de ser chiquitos no

le tienen miedo a casi nada.

Some pugs have jobs.
They go to hospitals
and nursing homes
to cheer people up.

Algunos pugs trabajan.
Van a los hospitales o a
las residencias de ancianos
para entretener a las personas.

From Puppy to Adult

Two to five pug puppies
are born in each litter.

De cachorro a adulto

Los pugs tienen de dos
a cinco cachorros en
cada camada.

Pug puppies like to play and chew. Chew toys help make their teeth strong.

A los cachorros pugs les gusta jugar y mordisquear cosas. Mordisquear juguetes les ayuda a tener dientes fuertes.

Adult pugs are small, strong dogs. They are as big as a large cat.

Los pugs adultos son pequeños y fuertes. Son del tamaño de un gato grande.

Pugs have short fur and
a curly tail. Their faces
are flat and wrinkled.

Los pugs son de pelo corto
y tiene la cola enroscada.
Sus caras son chatas
y arrugadas.

Taking Care of Pugs

Owners need to keep their pugs' faces clean. Dirt can get into the wrinkles.

Cómo cuidar a los pugs

Los dueños tienen que mantener limpia la cara de los pugs. La mugre puede metérseles entre las arrugas.

Pugs are house dogs.
They need to live indoors
and be warm and dry.

Los pugs son perros caseros.
Necesitan vivir adentro de
las casas y estar calientes
y secos.

Pugs need food, water, and exercise every day to stay healthy. Love from their owners keeps them happy.

Los pugs necesitan comida, agua y ejercicio todos los días para estar sanos. El cariño de sus dueños los hace felices.

Glossary

curly — curved into a circle

exercise — physical activity and movement done to stay healthy

hospital — a place where doctors and nurses help sick and hurt people

nursing home — a place where people live so that nurses and caregivers can take care of them

wrinkle — a line or crease

Internet Sites

FactHound offers a safe, fun way to find Internet sites related to this book. All of the sites on FactHound have been researched by our staff.

Here's how:

1. Visit *www.facthound.com*
2. Choose your grade level.
3. Type in this book ID **1429623861** for age-appropriate sites. You may also browse subjects by clicking on letters, or by clicking on pictures and words.
4. Click on the **Fetch It** button.

FactHound will fetch the best sites for you!

Glosario

la arruga — línea o pliegue

el ejercicio — actividad física y movimientos que se hacen para estar sano

enroscado — curva que forma un círculo

el hospital — lugar donde los doctores y enfermeras ayudan a los enfermos y heridos

la residencia de ancianos — lugar donde viven personas para que las enfermeras y cuidadores los atiendan

Sitios de Internet

FactHound te brinda una manera divertida y segura de encontrar sitios de Internet relacionados con este libro. Hemos investigado todos los sitios de FactHound. Es posible que algunos sitios no estén en español.

Se hace así:

1. Visita *www.facthound.com*
2. Elige tu grado escolar.
3. Introduce este código especial **1429623861** para ver sitios apropiados a tu edad, o usa una palabra relacionada con este libro para hacer una búsqueda general.
4. Haz un clic en el botón **Fetch It**.

¡FactHound buscará los mejores sitios para ti!

Index

Índice

Editorial Credits
Martha E. H. Rustad, editor; Katy Kudela, bilingual editor; Adalín Torres-Zayas,
    Spanish copy editor; Juliette Peters, designer; Wanda Winch, photo researcher;
    Scott Thoms, photo editor

Photo Credits
Corbis/Tim Davis, cover; Elite Portrait Design/Lisa Fallenstein-Holthaus, 6, 16, 18;
    Kent Dannen, 14; Mark Raycroft, 1, 4, 8, 20; Norvia Behling, 10; Ron Kimball Stock/
    Ron Kimball, 12